Singleton's Story
The Fylde's Model Village

By

Singleton History Group

Landy Publishing 2009

ISBN 978-1-872895-80-2

Layout by Sue Clarke
Printed by The Nayler Group, Church, Accrington. Tel: 01254 234247

INTRODUCTION

Lucky me! Of all the places my parents could have chosen to live they picked Little Singleton. My sister and I attended the village school under the care of Miss Travis and Miss Winckley. We joined in with Brownies, the Gala, and later, Singleton Cloggers. It was an idyllic childhood - and the start of an enjoyable lifetime in Singleton.

I have always had a passionate interest in local history and have enjoyed working with my fellow History Group members to create a wonderful archive of documents and photographs of Singleton village and its surrounding parish. Singleton Trust kindly allowed us to search through the Miller family estate documents and these helped us discover what life was like on the estate before and after Thomas Miller's purchase in 1853 of what was derelict and poorly managed land.

The 150th anniversary of the consecration of St Anne's Church gave us the ideal opportunity to put together a book that truly reflects the Singleton story. Our group has worked hard to gather together interesting photographs and snippets of a fascinating past. I hope you enjoy reading the book as much as we have enjoyed putting it together.

I am joined by the other members of the group in giving thanks to the Richard Dumbreck Singleton Trust; to Derek and Pam Hawthornthwaite who have spent days sorting all the information into a coherent story and writing most of the captions; to Clive Kidman for his scanning, editing and photography; to the other group members - Norma Clark, John and Olive Highton, Norma Jones, Judy Kay, Janet Pawson and Margaret Smith.

We want to acknowledge help received in various ways from Pat Allouis, Kathleen Angel (nee Evans), Greta Askew, John Bleazard, David Britton, Albert Clayton, Mary Cowell, Lisa Eland, *'The Evening Gazette'* staff, Lynda Inskip, Winnie Lee, Robin Percival, Norman Short, Alan and Ann Smith, Ann Turnbull, Roger and Adele Yeomans, the Lancashire Record Office staff and all other villagers who have supplied us with material.

Maxine Chew
November 2009

3

History of Singleton

The name *'Singleton'* probably derives from the Old English words *'shingle'*, meaning a wooden roof tile, and *'tun'*, meaning a farm or settlement. The parish of Singleton consists of about 2,923 acres, bounded on the north by the River Wyre, on the west by the Main Dyke, on the south by a stream called *'Lucas Flash'*, and in the east by the line of the A585 road, if extended to the Wyre at Windy Harbour.

In the Domesday Survey of 1086 the *'township'* of Singleton was assessed as containing six *'carucates'* of farmland, where one carucate equated to the amount that could be tilled by a plough and eight oxen in a year, probably 80-120 acres. It was held as *'demesne'* land by the Lords of the Honour of Lancaster: this meant that whoever held the earldom, later dukedom of Lancaster, counted Singleton as a portion of his personal property and could deal with it accordingly. Early in the 13th century, King John, the Duke of Lancaster, gave some Singleton land to the monks of Cockersand Abbey who collected rents from the eight tenants on their farmland (or *'grange'*) until King Henry dissolved the monasteries in 1538. The grange was bought by the Eccleston family of Great Eccleston.

After three generations they sub-divided and sold it. Further land in Singleton was granted in the 13th century to the family from Broughton Tower near Preston who held the hereditary office of *'Bailiffs of Amounderness'* (one of the Norman *'hundreds'* into which the country was divided.) They probably adopted the family name of *'de Singleton'* in honour of their holding. This land grant was the origin of Little Singleton. The principal house of the township was *'Mains Hall'* built on *'de Singleton'* land on a strategic site by the ford across the River Wyre at *'Aldwath'* (now Shard).

Great Singleton remained in the hands of the Honour and then Duchy of Lancaster, becoming Crown property in 1399. In 1623 it was sold, when King James 1 was short of money, as 'Singleton Magna' to Londoners William Weltden and Edward Badby, who sold it on in 1634 to London based William Fanshawe, Auditor to the Duchy of Lancaster and whose country home was at Parsloes, Essex. It remained in the Fanshawe family for more than a hundred years, until 1747, when it was bought by Prestonian William Shawe for £13,500. He married Ann Cunliffe, daughter of the MP for Liverpool. Their son, William Cunliffe Shawe, inherited it on his father's death in 1772 and lived at Singleton Lodge for a while.

Joseph Hornby, 1748-1832
(Picture by kind permission of Hugh Hornby and Peter Holme)

In 1803, Shawe sold the Great Singleton Estate to Joseph Hornby, a Kirkham sailcloth manufacturer, who much improved the estate, bought the windmill which stood on Weeton Road, re-built the Church and also rebuilt some farmhouses. His son and grandson inherited the estate in their turns.

William Fanshawe 1583-1634
(Picture by kind permission of London Borough of Barking and Dagenham)

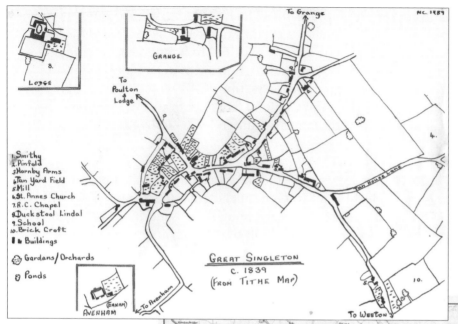

Two early maps showing how Great Singleton looked before Alderman Thomas Miller bought the land in 1853. The tithe map, reproduced with the permission of the County Archivist, Lancashire Record Office, is based on Singleton Tithe Plan (ref DRB/1/175)

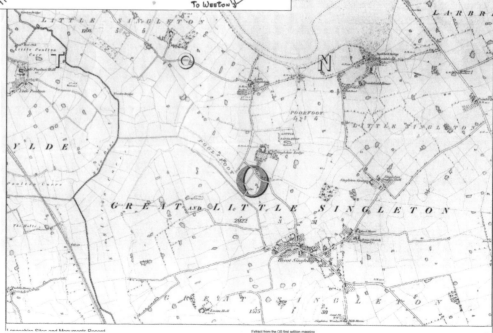

6

In 1853, Great Singleton was sold for £70,000 by Hugh Hilton Hornby to Alderman Thomas Miller of the Preston cotton manufacturers Horrocks-Miller. Alderman Thomas Miller was one of the most powerful and richest men in Preston at that time. He had a fashionable house in Winckley Square, Preston, and also a summer dwelling on West Beach, Lytham. Charles Dickens visited Preston on the first occasion when the cotton workers were on strike in 1853 and became friendly with Alderman Thomas. (It is alleged that he based his Book "*Hard Times*" on Miller and his factory workers.) Alderman Miller also bought land adjoining Singleton plus the Thistleton Estate. He used his fortune to demolish and rebuild Singleton and improve its agriculture. When he died, aged 54, in 1865, his eldest child, 19-year-old Thomas Horrocks Miller inherited the Singleton Estate and his second son, 16-year-old William Pitt Miller inherited Thistleton.

Alderman Thomas Miller
(Copyright of the Harris Museum
and Art Gallery Preston)

Thomas Horrocks Miller was destined for life as a country gentleman. He built Singleton Park in 1873 for his bride Isabel ('*Belle*') Armide Byrne, who he married in 1869. He and Belle remained childless. The year following her death in 1910 he married Issette Pearson of Putney, a prominent lady golfer. Thomas died in 1916 leaving Issette as life tenant of Singleton.

Thomas Horrocks Miller
(photo taken in his later years)

Photograph taken at a golf tournament around 1900 of Thomas ('*Tommy*') Miller with his first wife Belle (on the extreme left) and future wife Issette (in the middle, standing next to him!)

Following her death in 1941 the life tenancy passed to Thomas Pitt Miller, the 64-year-old son of William Pitt Miller. Thomas died in a Blackpool nursing home in 1945, and Singleton passed to his mentally and physically handicapped son, Thomas Humphrey Pitt Miller, who was incapable of living on his own. Singleton Park was sold at auction in 1946. Thomas died in the Royal Albert Hospital, Lancaster, in 1963, aged 43.

Adhering to Thomas Horrocks Miller's will of 1916, the Great Singleton Estate passed to the eldest grandson of his elder sister Henrietta, a man named Richard Dumbreck. An absentee, though caring, owner, Richard used the terms of his will to ensure the future of the estate. He died in 2003.

Issette Miller - Jessica Issette Frances Pearson - was born in Anglesey in 1861 and died in 1941. She survived Thomas Miller by 25 years and continued to run Singleton Estate with an iron fist. Running the estate needed some determination, and so to some of the villagers she appeared to be a tyrant, but deep down she was quite a thoughtful and caring person, providing the village with many facilities and helping residents with many of their needs. She was the founder member of the Ladies Golf Union and became its Honorary Secretary. Some of her male contemporaries preferred to call her the Czar of Golf!

Issette was instrumental in devising the sport's handicapping system, originally by placing women into three categories according to their ability. The British Men's Golfing Authority thought it was a ridiculous idea, but when the United States Golfing Association adopted it for both men and women the British had to accept that Issette was right and adopted the scheme.

The Fire Station, c1906, the most famous landmark of Singleton. Thomas Horrocks Miller built the fire station in the village in 1882. It had a team of 14 volunteers, a captain, one horse drawn manual engine and, of course, a horse which presumably grazed in the nearby field. It is said the horse was an unwilling member of the National Fire Brigade Union and did not turn up for duty willingly!

Copy of the back sheet of a deed drawn up on the 23rd October 1851 separating the '*townships*' of Great Singleton and Little Singleton from the hamlet of Thistleton, which became a parish in its own right.

Another picture of Singleton Fire Station taken a few years later. The fire station became redundant and the fire engine was actually sold in 1946 with the contents of Singleton Park. The building is presently used as an electricity sub-station. The fire station is worthy of closer inspection for its elaborate architecture - it really is a pretty little building: the '*Tudor*' plasterwork is engraved with many plants and flowers, and the gutters on the right-hand side are unusual in sporting lions' heads.

Singleton Fire Brigade minus the horse! Posing after a fire at Elswick in 1906.

Part of the National Fire Brigade Union Drill Book of 1894 showing that it has been stamped by Singleton Parish Council on the 3rd October 1899 (but no mention here about catching the horse!)

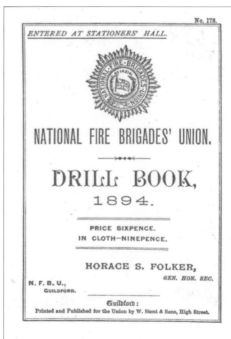

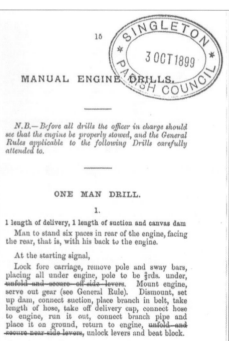

ENTERED AT STATIONERS' HALL.

No. 178.

NATIONAL FIRE BRIGADES' UNION.

DRILL BOOK,
1894.

PRICE SIXPENCE.
IN CLOTH—NINEPENCE.

HORACE S. FOLKER,
GEN. HON. SEC.

N. F. B. U.,
GUILDFORD.

Guildford:
Printed and Published for the Union by W. Stent & Sons, High Street.

15

SINGLETON
PARISH COUNCIL
3 OCT 1899

MANUAL ENGINE DRILLS.

N.B.—Before all drills the officer in charge should see that the engine be properly stowed, and the General Rules applicable to the following Drills carefully attended to.

ONE MAN DRILL.

1.

1 length of delivery, 1 length of suction and canvas dam

Man to stand six paces in rear of the engine, facing the rear, that is, with his back to the engine.

At the starting signal,

Lock fore carriage, remove pole and sway bars, placing all under engine, pole to be ⅔rds. under, unfold and secure off side levers. Mount engine, serve out gear (see General Rule). Dismount, set up dam, connect suction, place branch in belt, take length of hose, take off delivery cap, connect hose to engine, run it out, connect branch pipe and place it on ground, return to engine, unfold and secure near side levers, unlock levers and beat block.

11

Singleton's pub was originally called the *'Hornby Arms'*, until Thomas Miller bought the village in 1853. He renamed it the *'Miller Arms'*, placing his coat of arms over the front door with his motto,*' Sibimet Merces Industria'*, which means industry is a recompense to itself. This was painted by the pre-Raphaelite artist Leopold Egg (1816-1863).

The Miller Arms was a working farm with stables, shippons, pig sties and land attached. There was also a well, which is under the present building. However, a pub is always the centre of village life, and Singleton's was no exception, with horse-drawn wagons providing day trips from Blackpool, and events such as weddings, christenings and funerals also catered for. Darts and dominos were played and

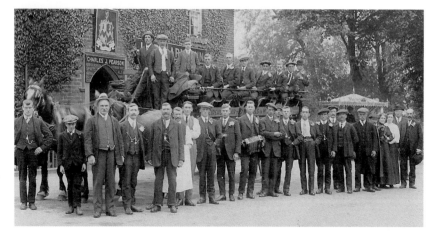

silver cups presented, usually on evenings boasting hot-pot suppers. The inn was used by local farmers to pay their rent on Rent Days, and ploughing matches were held in the field opposite. After a day's shoot visitors and villagers would retire to the pub for supper and plenty of drink.

Present-day visitors may note that after many years of being rendered and whitewashed the Miller Arms has been sandblasted to expose its original brickwork - not so dissimilar to this early twentieth century photograph.

Florence Helen Sharp pulling pints in the Miller Arms. She, with her husband Joshua Septimus, were tenants from 1914 to 1928, when the tenancy was taken over by their daughter Enid and her husband, Tom Eaves.

The letter heading promoting Puck Matches was a new idea for advertising both the hotel and the matches.

View taken from the Miller Arms towards the Manor Farm junction. The white house on the left was originally one house (known as *'Gillows Farm'*} and later converted into three cottages and demolished in the late 1950s because of their bad state of repair. The house, if still standing, would have been worth a blue plaque as it was the birthplace in 1704 of Robert Gillow, who founded the Lancaster-based high-class furniture firm of Gillows. Records show the Gillows were still occupying the farm in 1839.

This view looks from Weeton Road (formerly Mill Lane). In the background is Manor Farm, a larger and more prestigious farmhouse than Gillow Farm.

Miller date stone on Manor Farm showing the intertwined initials of T.H. Miller 1899.

Singleton Windmill, which stood on Weeton Road, became part of the Great Singleton Estate in 1807 when Joseph Hornby, the then owner of the Estate, bought it from the Gorst family, owners of Preese Hall, for £144. From the late 1850s it was tenanted by the Clark family, who in 1915 installed an oil engine to replace the sails. By World War 2 the mill needed repair and was sold by the Miller Estate although the Clarks continued as tenants, latterly using the mill for storage. Daniel Clark, who had been the last miller, died in 1948. Peggy (nee Clark) and her husband Charles Sewell left the mill in 1956. The new owners moved into the mill house but demolished the mill in the late 1950s.

SINGLETON WIND MILL

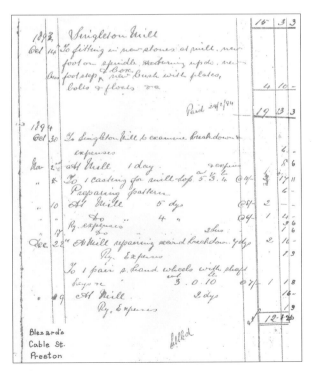

Singleton Windmill invoice, dated 1893, relating to repairs to the mill.

Views of the centre of the village, including one of Worswick Farm.

Postcard written and posted on the 20th September 1938 by C. Dyson with an 'awful pen' whilst staying with Mrs. Sandham at Worswick Farm. The 'Jimmie' he refers to is his parrot, which he says he could have brought with him for company for Mrs. Sandham's parrot!

Tranquil life in the centre of Singleton. The photograph was taken in the early 1900s and was still being used for postcards, like this one, in 1932.

16

These photographs are of the same house in the centre of the Village. The earlier photo, when the house was brick and a Post Office, was taken in the early 1900s. (See pages 24 & 25 for sites of the Post Office). In the 1940s the house was used by the garage/blacksmith proprietor so in essence was the *'Smithy Cottage'*. The later photo shows the house whitewashed in the 1980s, when it was the *'Old Smithy Cottage'* and the smithy next door had been upgraded to a motor garage, advertising Fina petrol at 73p for two star and 74p for four star - per gallon!

Singleton Service Station occupies the site of the 19th Century village smithy. Earlier it was where the fire station is now. This photograph was taken about 1946 when Lloyd George Evans was the owner, and his sign indicates the garage also dealt with agricultural engineering, and shoeing, as well as general smith work. He was proud of the sign as the style of lettering reminded him of his favourite *'Senior Service'* cigarettes.

This photo of Singleton Blacksmiths taken in the early 1900s shows Billy Haslem on the right with his apprentice John Willie Jackson on the left. John Jackson later became the proprietor of the Singleton Service Station prior to Mr. Evans in the early 1940s.

This fingerpost at the junction of Station Road and Lodge Lane still indicates the A585 runs through the centre of the village, which it did until the by-pass was built in the 1970s.

Singleton Service Station circa 1970s. This was taken before the previous photograph and shows Green Shield Stamps were being given away! The garage's service bay is where the village Reading Room once stood and the wooden hut in the background was once part of it. At the time of this photograph the hut was still used as a reading room but it has since been dismantled, leaving only a small section, used in the past by Mr. Parkinson as a joinery workshop.

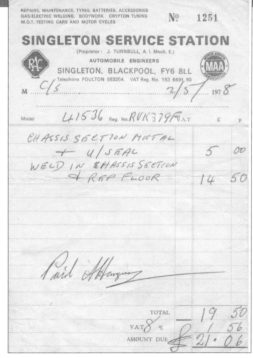

Singleton Service Station letterheaded paper and a bill when Mr. J. Turnbull was the proprietor. The bill is dated the 2nd May 1978 when repair work looks very cheap and VAT was only 8%! It is signed by Alan Hargreaves, the foreman mechanic.

Quaint photograph, taken in the early 1900s, showing perhaps a father and daughter walking in the village. The black-and-white timber building, which once stood by the smithy, is the Reading Room built by Mr. Miller as a meeting room for his male estate workers and villagers. Newspapers and books were provided and there was also a billiard table. During the 1930s part of the front of this L-shaped structure was dismantled and a smaller timber building was left for community use. When the Queen's coronation in 1953 was broadcast a television was installed in the meeting room so villagers could watch the event together and enjoy a party.

Photograph of the cottages in the village adjacent to the white cottages in the previous photo.

Newspaper cuttings relating to events held in the Parochial Hall in the 1920s.

Singleton Bowling Club on President's Day, showing Bill Smith starting the Miller Cup Final. The bowling green adjoining the Parochial Hall was given to the villagers by Issette Miller in 1924.

One of two cups at the first Singleton Bowling Green event, won by Joshua Septimus Sharp in 1925. An identical cup was won by his son-in-law, Tom Eaves, in 1930. Mr. Sharp and Mr. Eaves were landlords of the Miller Arms.

SINGLETON

A jumble sale held in the Singleton Church Hall on Saturday, realised over £7.

The proceeds were on behalf of the Singleton Nursing Association, and much satisfaction was felt over the good response of the public in support of the cause, the sum raised being larger than results obtained for the same object on previous occasions.

Mrs. Miller, of Singleton Park, who had not been in the best of health for some time past, had sufficiently recovered to enable her to attend and open the sale.

She was accompanied by Mrs. Watson, wife of the Vicar of Singleton, and both ladies appealed for liberal support.

Singleton is to have its customary Children's Gala Day. The committee which met in the Church Hall on Wednesday under the chairmanship of the Rev. T. H. Watson, Vicar of Singleton, felt that the war should not deprive the children of the joy of their annual carnival and fixed upon Wednesday, June 19th, for the event.

There is to be as far as possible a pre-war programme, with the time-honoured ceremony of the crowning of the Rose Queen.

Who the Rose Queen is to be is not yet determined.

The selection will be made by the school children of the village.

May 1940 newspaper cutting about a jumble sale in the Church Hall.

One of the many wells in Singleton, this was uncovered in 2005 while creating a children's play area, now known as *'Miller Park'*, adjacent to the bowling green.

A lovely photograph of the Post Office showing the old wooden fingerpost - now on the corner of a very busy mini roundabout! (This photograph was taken before the pillar box and path were installed on the Station Road side. Entry to the shop then was on Lodge Lane.)

The Old Vicarage. Behind this house was the site of the last Roman Catholic Chapel in Singleton. Built in 1771, the chapel was still being used in 1814, but problems over the renewal of the lease meant St. John's Church in Breck Road, Poulton-le-Fylde, was used instead. The chapel was re-opened in 1831 when a lease had been secured, and was sold in 1861 to Mr. Frederick Earnshaw Marshall, of Penwortham, with the proviso that it was demolished within twelve months. The bell believed to have come from the chapel is now at St. John's. It is understood that the left-hand side of The Old Vicarage could have formed part of the priest's house.

Various photographs of where the Post Office has been located. One photo shows the small white cottage in the middle which was originally the smithy cottage, a back door giving entry to some smithy buildings. At some stage this became an early Post Office: now that the whitewash is disappearing off the lintel of the front left window the remains of the POST OFFICE lettering can be seen.

An early postcard to Miss Brierley at Poulton from Sallie, posted with a Great Singleton stamp on the 2nd July 1905, while Sallie was staying at Mrs. Porter's, the second white house on Church Road.

24

The Post Office moved from the old white cottage to this building (now the garage house), as this 1911 photo shows.

The Post Office moved again, to the present shop, as we can see from this postcard, posted in 1938.

An unusual plant flowering in the Postmaster's garden was exciting news, according to this 1930s newspaper cutting!

SINGLETON.

An unusual plant is flowering in a Singleton garden. It is a blue poppy and has been raised from seed by Mr. H. Mapp, of Singleton Post Office. There are three blooms on the poppy and it is doubtful if there are any other flowers of its kind in the Fylde with the exception of a few at Singleton Park.

Looking up Station Road, with the first cottage after the Post Office being marked as the Police Station.

Another view up Station Road, showing an old *'Low Bridge'* sign on the left.

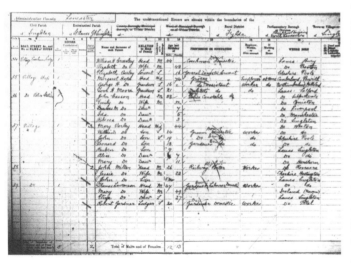

Copy of the 1901 census. Interestingly, of the 25 people listed on this sheet only 6 were born in Singleton! The census starts with Mr. Crossley the coachman, his wife and servant residing at the Coachhouse Lodge. In the village shop is Margaret Hope, widow, a grocer with the help of her two grandsons. Moving up Station Road at the Police Station is PC John Casson, plus his wife and three daughters. (His job certainly made his family move - one daughter was born in Liverpool, another in Manchester, and the last in Singleton.) At the next cottage along the road was Mary Varley, widow, her four sons and three daughters - her sons being grooms and a gardener. Two of her daughters were born in Singleton. Next is John Miller, railway porter, his wife and 5-month old son, who was born in Singleton. Next is Thomas Lawrenson, a gardener and domestic labourer, born in Singleton; his wife and daughter also born in Singleton; together with a lodger, Robert Gardner, a gardener.

26

This photo shows, in the middle of the picture, the Old Vicarage which is now hidden by mature trees.

Another photograph looking down Station Road towards The Village.

Looking up Station Road on a sunny day in 1938.

Taken at the entrance of Mount Farm looking down Station Road towards The Village. The land to the right was purchased in the early 1970s by Mini Con for the development of four houses called *'The Beeches'*.

Another Singleton well was found while Mini Con were preparing *'The Beeches'* site. The inquisitive little boy is John Bleazard's son, Stephen.

Estate cottages on Station Road.

Buildings to the rear of these cottages included workshop for the trades required to maintain all buildings on the estate - including joiners, wheelwrights, and plumbers - and is still used today as a workshop. Winston Parkinson, who still works in the workshop, has lovely memories of boyish pranks and games played on the estate. He and his friend used to go into the Park and call the shire horses over: they would then shout and wave their arms to frighten them and watch with glee as they galloped round the field. Issette Miller was not amused with this prank and would often catch them. She would raise her cane over their outspread hands, pulling up inches short before hitting them, as a lesson not to do it again. When asked did they do it again, Winston said *"Yes"*!!

Behind this building were the estate's kennels, where the pack of hunting hounds were kept.

This 'cottage' on Carr Lane was built by Alderman Thomas Miller as a little country retreat for his wife: it was later called 'Knowle House' and then 'Mallard Hall'. They did have a 'summer cottage' on West Beach at Lytham but Mr. Miller wanted a home on his estate at Singleton. The 'cottage', which to judge from this picture has been newly built and is in pristine condition, was not grand enough for Mrs. Henrietta Miller and they never did live in it. It was instead used by the estate manager and his wife.

Another photo of 'The Cottage', showing a few extensions and the large garden pond.

MAY 1941

SINGLETON

The funeral took place at Singleton Parish Church on Tuesday, of Mrs. Winifred Mary Procter, the wife of Mr. Lionel Procter, of Knowle House, Singleton, the agent for the Singleton estates, who died after a short illness on Sunday.

Coming to Singleton with her husband about a year ago, Mrs. Procter, who was 46 years of age, had won all hearts by her charming personality and happy disposition.

She took a keen interest in the welfare of movements in the village, and had been keenly and actively interested in the women's war work.

She leaves a husband and one son, to whom general sympathy will be extended.

The funeral service was conducted by the Vicar, the Rev. T. H. Watson, and in addition to members of the family there was a large attendance of friends at the church.

Wreaths were sent by:

Husband; Leo (son); Mamma and Dada; Durston and May; Mr. Procter (father-in-law); Uncle Will and Auntie Nellie; Lennox and Mara; Mr. and Mrs. Russell; Mr. and Mrs. J. Whalley; Wood Yard staff; Singleton schoolchildren; Squadron Ldr Maclaughlan; Mrs Frampton; Mr. and Mrs. Jennay and family; Nurse Lowry; Mrs. Fellows; Mr. and Mrs. Stephenson; Kenneth Farnworth; Margaret Whitehead.

Mr. and Mrs. W. L. Jones; Mrs. Steyning; Mrs. Chivnall; Women War Workers of Singleton; Mr. and Mrs. Pierce; Mr. and Mrs. W. L. Low; Margery, Ernest and Ruth; Molly; Mr. and Mrs. Eastham.

Mrs. Marginson; Staff at Singleton Park; Rev. T. H. and Mrs Watson; Mr. and Mrs. T. Smith; Harold and Dora; tenant farmers of Singleton; Percy and Dorie.

A May 1941 newspaper cutting about the funeral of Mrs. Winifred Mary Proctor, the wife of Lionel Proctor, of 'Knowle House' (formerly known as 'The Cottage'), who was agent for the Singleton Estate.

Not every train stopped at Singleton Station, as may be noted from the newspaper cutting. (Plans to extend the station and buildings never came to anything.) When Mr. Miller came to Singleton, Station Road did not run all the way to the railway line but terminated at Avenham Hall. He asked the council for the road to be made up to Hardhorn, making access to the station much easier. Mr. Miller had

most of his house guests alight at Singleton Station and they would think nothing of walking all the way to the Hall. One would hope that his servants would have placed the guests' heavy bags on a waggonette!

This '*Preston Pilot*' newspaper cutting, dated 5th September 1883, described a fatal leap - one of the instances where the train did not stop at Singleton Station and William Turner thought that he could just jump off and run home: he died at home from his injuries.

FATAL LEAP FROM A RAILWAY TRAIN.—On Saturday morning there died at his residence at Singleton, near Poulton-le-Fylde, William Turner, pointsman in the Singleton cabin, who sacrificed his life in a foolish attempt to drop from a passenger train whilst it was running at a speed of about 40 miles per hour. The deceased had been with his brother to Preston, and they returned by the 9-45 p.m. train. When near Singleton, the deceased, thinking he could safely drop from the train, and save a walk from Poulton, the next stopping place, got out of the compartment, and at Singleton leaped off. As soon as his foot touched the ground he bounded for over 15 yards, and alighted on his head. His brother saw the accident, but could not stop the train. He afterwards returned to the place, and found his brother lying insensible. He had him conveyed home, when Dr. Winn was called in, and that gentleman found him suffering from concussion of the brain and paralysis. He died on Saturday.

Singleton Station to be Closed

Singleton railway station will be closed to passenger traffic on and after next Monday. All goods traffic, apart from bulk coal and minerals, will be dealt with at Poulton.

The frequent bus service between Blackpool and Garstang, with connections to Preston, is the cause of the railway company's decision. Six trains from Preston and five from Blackpool call daily at Singleton station which is some distance from the village, but there is an hourly bus service passing through the village between Blackpool and Garstang.

The railway station has been in use for more than 50 years.

This 1932 newspaper cutting reported that Singleton Railway Station was to be closed after 50 years'

Singleton Station Signal Box, photographed in the 1960s, and now long gone.

Singleton Signal Box c.1960's

Two sorts of horse power from times gone by! One photo, taken at Singleton Railway Bridge when its arch had an 8-foot headroom, is of Bob Houseman of Oldfield Carr Farm, Poulton-le-Fylde, with his horse and cart. The other photograph, taken in August 1959, is of John Whalley, of Fairfield Farm, with his tractor and load.

A *'T.H. Miller'* date stone of 1890 at Avenham Hall, Station Road. The farm was originally called *'Enam Hall'* and renamed Avenham Hall by T.H. Miller.

'Family Tree' of the Miller family, showing how Thomas Horrocks Miller's line died out and the estate was passed down his sister's side, ending up with Richard Dumbreck of Sussex overseeing the estate. Singleton Trust was set up following Mr. Dumbreck's death.

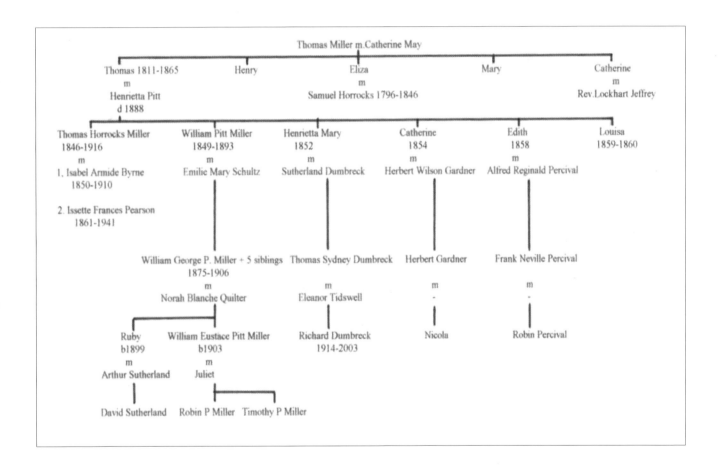

Various photographs showing Singleton Park in its hey day. It was built in 1873 by T.H. Miller. Upon Issette Miller's death the park house passed to Thomas Pitt Miller, and on his death in 1945 it passed to his son, Thomas Humphrey Pitt Miller. The contents of the hall were sold at a sale in 1946 and the hall itself was later sold to Lancashire County Council. In 1952 it was a special school for physically handicapped boys.

With sincere wishes
for your happiness at Christmas
and
throughout the New Year.

SINGLETON PARK.

A personalised Christmas card from Issette Miller, of Singleton Park, sent probably in the 1930s.

This 'Preston Pilot' newspaper cutting, dated 30th August 1882, reported Mr. T.H. Miller winning first prizes at the Lancaster Agricultural Show. In 1870 Mr. Miller had become a member of the Royal Agricultural Society. He was later elected to its council and remained a representative for 32 years. His farming abilities were quite famous in the Fylde, and on 12th December 1883 his ensilage silo at Singleton Park was opened.

> T. H. MILLER, Esq., Singleton Park, took the first prize for a shearling ram, and the first prize for a pen of three one shear gimmers (not having been fed for the butcher), and the first prize for three gimmer lambs (not fed for the butcher) at the Lancaster Agricultural Show.

The fire station brings some lovely colour to this Autumn photograph.

Francesca Britton,
Rose Queen in 2000.

Singleton Cloggers, taken in the early 1980s. The Cloggers' board leader is Daniel West. Those recognised are - left-hand line: Ann Smith; middle line, going backwards: Tom Nolan, Joan Taziker, Jane West, David Kay and John Chew; right-hand line: Maxine Chew and, behind her, Dick West.

Singleton School taken in summer months.

The redundant postbox, in the Post Office porch was installed during the reign of King George the Sixth.

The present postbox, on Station Road outside the Post Office bears the motif of Queen Elizabeth who came to the throne in 1952.

The original Singleton Park gates can be seen, still in situ, by the side of the South Lodge.

This Dumbreck Court sign came into use in 2009. The name is explained on page 71.

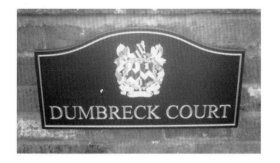

The country lane running behind Church Road

Pictured is the Parochial Hall or Village Hall or Church Hall, erected in 1924 at the insistance of Issette Miller, which still looks the same as the day it was built.

The beautiful tiles in the chancel of St. Anne's Church.

General view of the altar at St. Anne's Church.

Stained-glass window in the South transept showing the cotton flowers which were connected with Alderman Thomas Miller's cotton business.

In 2004 a team of embroiderers from St Chad's, Poulton and St Anne's, Singleton, worked to produce the vestments of which this is a section. Kathleen Angell (nee Evans), bought the vestments for the church in memory of her parents and brother who owned Singleton smithy and service station.

Singleton Park, almost covered in ivy, about 1910.

A newspaper cutting, from the 'Preston Pilot' dated 15th September 1880, promoting Singleton Fair for the sale of pedigree Shropshire sheep. (Note that arrangements had been made for the train to stop at Singleton Station.)

Sales by Auction.

SHROPSHIRE DOWN SHEEP.
The Fifth Annual Sale by Auction of Pure-bred SHROPSHIRE DOWN SHEEP, the property of Thomas Horrocks Miller, Esquire, of Singleton Park, Poulton-le-Fylde, will be held at Singleton Fair on Thursday, 21st September, 1882, and will comprise
FIVE SHEARLING RAMS,
30 RAM LAMBS,
24 SHEARLING and STOCK EWES.
These Sheep have been most carefully bred from some of the most noted flocks in existence, including those of the late Lord Chesham, Mrs. Beach, Messrs. Byrd, Coxon, Evans, Smith, Williams Minton, and others, and have been most successful in the show-yard.
Singleton is one mile from Singleton Station, and two and a half miles from Poulton Station, Preston and Wyre Railway. By permission of the Company the train leaving Preston at 12 30, and that leaving Poulton at 5 24, will stop at Singleton Station to set down and take up passengers attending the sale, which will commence at two o'clock.—Catalogues and further particulars may be obtained from the Auctioneer, Mr. Ashcroft, Lancaster-road, Preston.

The 1901 census records Thomas Horrocks Miller as a *'Landed Proprietor'* together with his wife Isabel living in the hall with nine servants, none whom were born in Singleton! - a housekeeper, butler, ladies' maid, two kitchen maids, two house maids and two laundry maids. In *'Garden Lodge'* were two gardeners. In *'North Lodge'* lived Mr. Cardwell, head gardener, with his wife and two daughters who were born in Singleton together with Mr. Cardwell's mother. In *'Gate Lodge'* resided William Reeves, a coachman and his wife, two daughters and two sons - one of whom was a groom.

Proof that the landed gentry could have their names embossed on every brick that their house was built with! Thistleton Brick and Tile Works, which was next to Fisher's Slack Cottage, was active at this time, but it is unlikely that these Miller bricks would have been fired there.

THM's initials were on everything - including the Park gates.

Front cover from the Sale Catalogue of the contents of Singleton Park. The sale was held over four days in April 1946 and there were more than 1,343 lots including antiques, exquisite furniture, solid silver articles, Dresden and Crown Derby china. Some very interesting wine was in the sale - one including a 1-gallon jar of potent proof whisky spirit sealed in 1570! Everything which had remained at the Park was in the sale - down to bedding, mattresses, pots, pans, string fruit netting, gardening tools and, in the garage, a 1938 Humber Snipe 25 hp motor car and an early stage coach. All his artwork, including paintings by Turner, Landseer, Constable, and the pre-Raphaelites, were sold at a separate auction held at the end of April 1946.

Newspaper cutting dated May 1901 depicting a wonderful account of a party for scholars held upon the '*turf*' in the front of Singleton Park.

SINGLETON.

Upon the turf in front of Singleton Hall, upwards of one hundred bright, rosy-cheeked children, on Tuesday, romped and tumbled, whilst their joyous shouts and rippling laughter echoed and re-echoed through the plantations round about the residence of Mr. and Mrs. T. H. Miller. These were the scholars attending the Sunday School classes started by Miss Wood, daughter of the Rev. L. C. Wood, about a year ago, and they were then enjoying the pleasures of their first treat. Tea was provided in a manner which gave the utmost joy to the youngsters, the donors being Mesdames T. Jackson, Martindale, Shepherd, Richardson, E. Richardson, E. Clark, and James. Mrs. G. Nutter gave the tea to the teachers and visitors. Games of all kinds were arranged for the children, and later they assembled in front of the hall, where Mrs. Miller presented the children with handsome prizes for their regular attendance at the Sunday School. The recipients were :—Miss Woods' class: Isabel Dodgson, R. Hubert, A. Richardson, Jane Winchester, Jessie Howe, H. Martindale. Mr. Luther's class: E. Richardson, R. Richardson, S. James, W. Ronson, L. Varley, J. W. Jackson, A. Kay, and S. Richardson. Mrs. Mapp's class: Annie Porter, Nellie Clarke, A. Kay, E. Winchester, K. Tuson, H. Ronson. Miss Richardson's class: B. Hull, Ivy Jackson, F. Casson, Marie Nutter, Lizzie Kay, and May Jackson. Mrs. Hope's class: Jno. Ronson, S. Mapp, A. Hull, W. Hope, and E. Richardson. The thankfulness of the scholars to Mr. and Mrs. Miller was expressed by three hearty cheers, and then, under the superintendence of Mr. T. Phillips, day schoolmaster, they sang several songs. The festivities were concluded with a supper, also given by the above-mentioned donors. The school has an attendance of about 80 children each Sunday, and is under the superintendence of Mr. W. Luther. An active part in the Sunday School work is taken by Miss Wood, who is assisted by about five teachers. The last Government report received on the work at the Singleton day school states that " the present teacher has made an excellent start in his evening school, and the results of the work are very encouraging. The regularity and the intelligent interest of the scholars deserve special praise." The average attendance at the school is now 95 per cent., and everything points to Mr. Phillips, the new headmaster, making a great success.

Newspapers in July 1912 reported the tragic drowning at Pittfield Farm of two children - Mary Jane Cowell (10) and Anthony Bond (6). The incident upset Issette Miller so much that she offered to let her swimming pool at Singleton Park be used by all the local children to help them learn to swim.

Arthur Mee published a little verse relating to the drowning in his book *One Thousand Beautiful Things*, called *A Little Girl's Goodnight*:

> *"From a village in Lancashire comes a story with a courage and a love*
> *in it too deep for words. The boy and girl were bathing with other*
> *children in a pond on a farm at Singleton, when the boy aged 6 found*
> *himself beyond his depth. His cousin swam out to save him but she too*
> *went beyond her depth, and the boy and girl were drowned. Helpless*
> *on the banks stood their grief stricken playmates. The brave little girl*
> *as she rose to the surface for the last time called out to them*
> *'Goodnight'.*

November 21st 1880
Preston Pilot
COVER SHOOTING AT SINGLETON PARK -Last week, on Tuesday,
Wednesday and Thursday, there were three days cover shooting
on T.H. Miller Esq's estates at Singleton and the following
was the total results - 513 pheasants   23 partridges, 793
hares, 53 rabbits, 4 woodcocks, 1 duck, 18 various, and 1
trout; total 1406

A newspaper cutting from the 'Preston Pilot' reporting a good days shooting - amusingly including one trout!

Singleton Park's Coach House, on the south side of the main drive.

'Honest Tom's' grave in the grounds of Singleton Park. Honest Tom was Thomas H Miller's champion stallion shire horse. Miller boasted that he stacked 500 gold sovereigns on the table to buy this horse, which won many prizes and cups during its lifetime. A pair of tankards engraved with the name Honest Tom were listed in the Auction Sale Catalogue of 1946.

'Honest Tom's' body was buried in the grave but his head was stuffed and mounted and thereafter displayed firstly at Preston Town Hall and then at the Preston Cattle Market. His head 'disappeared' when the market building was demolished to make way for housing. Other graves shared with 'Honest Tom' were those of the Miller's beloved family pets: one was 'Spot', which used to have on his collar disc 'Touch me not, But let me jog, For I am Spot, Tom Miller's dog - Singleton Park'.

A painting of 'Honest Tom', with Singleton Park in the background, copied by Pat Allouis from the original oil-painting by Basil Bradley.

The Ice House at Singleton Park with a person unknown entering the gloom. The Ice House was used before there were refrigerators: in winter, ice was taken from the nearby pond and stored in this underground vault for use later in the year.

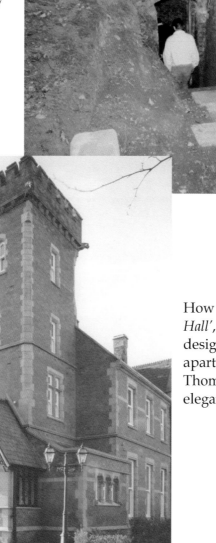

How *'Singleton Park'*, now called *'Singleton Hall'*, looks today. The hall has been re-designed and transformed into several apartments: it still looks imposing and Thomas H. Miller would be proud that its elegance has been retained.

1920s postcard showing the North Lodge, on Lodge Lane, which has since been extended and is now privately owned.

The 1881 census record of the occupants of Lodge Farm: Scotland-born Robert Gardiner was the head of the farm and living with his wife, four daughters and one son, all of them born in Singleton. There were two female and three male servants.

Annie Martindale (later Smith) of Lodge Farm. Before
the photo was taken Annie had been to the Farmers' Ball,
and it must have been a good one, because she arrived
home just in time to put on her bonnet and smock over
her *'going-out'* clothes ready to milk Daisy!

The *'Roundhouse'* at Lodge Farm in 1967.
It was demolished in the 1970s. The
roundhouse was used to grind corn,
usually for animal feed: a horse was
harnessed to walk round and round
turning gears which turned the grinding
stones. The sides of the building would
have been open to the elements but this
photo shows the sides bricked up: by
this time the building would have been
used for storage.

'*Singleton Lodge*', formerly '*The Vicarage*', an attractive Georgian-style property adjoining Lodge Farm farmhouse. William Cunliffe Shaw lived there in 1786 and later rented it out. In 1803 the estate was sold to Joseph Hornby, of Ribby Hall, a linen merchant of Kirkham.

In 1809 the property was used as a vicarage. The Reverend Thomas Banks, a vicar of Singleton, resided there and for some time ran a boarding school. In 1843, the next vicar appointed was the Reverend Leonard Charles Wood who died in office in 1911 aged 92 leaving his unmarried children to reside at the Lodge until the last of them, Mary Eleanor, died in 1935.

In 1935 '*Singleton Lodge*' was the home of the Frampton family, Mr. Frampton being the harbour master at Fleetwood. The next harbour master, Commander Powell, lived there in the 1950s. The next occupants were Mr. Lyness, a school inspector, and his family: they bought the tenancy in the 1960s when the Singleton Estate was offered for sale.

Alan and Ann Smith bought Singleton Lodge and have developed it into a successful hotel and restaurant. In the 1990s, Lodge Farm farmhouse was incorporated into Singleton Lodge in order to extend it. The beautiful gardens are bounded on the south side by a '*ha-ha*' which is a ditch with a wall on its inner side below ground level forming a boundary without interrupting the view. Singleton has three ha-ha's - at Singleton Lodge, Singleton Hall, and Mallard Hall.

RATEPAYERS' MEETING AT SINGLETON.—At a meeting held on Tuesday, the Rev. L. C. Wood in the chair, the officials appointed were:—Messrs. R Charnley and R Baxter, overseers; guardian, Mr. J. Lawson; assessors and collectors of Queen's taxes, Messrs. J. Clarke and J. Livesey; surveyor for Great Singleton, Mr. J. Livesey, and for Little Singleton, Mr. R. Catterall. A vote of thanks to the chairman brought the meeting to a close.

'*Preston Pilot*' newspaper cutting, dated 29th March 1882, relating to a Ratepayers Meeting at Singleton being chaired by the Rev. L. C. Wood.

A turn of the century postcard showing the Singleton Lodge vicarage and a photo of Rev. Wood.

'*Preston Pilot*' newspaper cutting, dated 10th September 1882, reporting the death of the Rev. L. C. Wood's wife Sophia.

DEATHS.
On Sept. 10th, at Singleton Vicarage, Sophia, wife of the Rev. Leonard Charles Wood, Vicar of Singleton.

Photo of '*South Lodge*', on Lodge Lane, which is now privately owned and has been sympathetically extended.

A hidden architectural gem in Singleton: South Lodge has a unique stone sculpture of a dog's head, at eaves level on the left hand corner as can be seen in the previous photo. Whether this was one of Miller dogs or the stonemason's, we may never know.

Two views, looking up
Church Road, about 1904.

It is believed that the original Singleton School was situated very close to where St. Anne's Church now stands.

The present Singleton Village Day School on Church Road was built in 1863 by Alderman Thomas Miller to accommodate 100 pupils. There were two classrooms, one for juniors and one for seniors, with boys and girls having separate entrances and play yards and earth toilets in the

yard. The original open fireplace still exists in the main hall. Across the road was the school garden where pupils learned the skills of growing produce and tending a garden. This photo from the early 1900s shows the children with their teacher in the garden. The only pupil we can name is Jane Cowell, the lovely girl dressed in dark with a white ribbon in her hair. Issette Miller took a great interest in village activities. Sometimes she would arrive at the school unannounced and hand pick pupils to assist as gardeners, domestic staff or farm workers.

In 1952 the school was transferred to the Blackburn Diocesan Board and thereafter children were transferred at the age of 11 to secondary school. Until then children had received the whole of their education at Singleton. Over the years the school has been enlarged, the first extension, in 1959, providing two more classrooms and flushing lavatories! It cost around £1,000, with the Church paying half. A foundation stone was laid by Mrs. Jane Cowell of Pittfield Farm.

To this day pupils who attend Singleton School still benefit from the beautiful rural location, surrounded by fields and trees. The school has a playing field and a peaceful woodland area, donated by the Richard Dumbreck Singleton Trust.

Photo, taken about 1908, of schoolchildren and two teachers at Singleton School.

'Preston Pilot' newspaper cutting, dated 21st August 1878, reporting on a school outing to Lytham.

How many children playing at the front of school looked up and saw this lovely stone sculpture of a rabbit? Why it is there is anybody's guess - perhaps a stonemason's favourite?

SINGLETON SCHOOLS EXCURSION.—On Friday last the children belonging to the Day and Sunday Schools of the united parishes of Singleton and Thistleton enjoyed a delightful excursion to Lytham, where they spent the day. The members of the choir of Singleton Church were also of the party, which altogether numbered over a hundred, who were conveyed to Lytham by road in eight conveyances, the whole expenses of the day, both as regards transit and of dinner, tea, and all refreshments at Lytham, being kindly defrayed by T. H. Miller, Esq., of Singleton Park. Driving direct to the Clifton Arms Hotel the party then speedily made their way to the beach and shore, and it was amusing to see the delight of the children as they came in sight of the sea, it being high tide at the time, with steamers and pleasure boats moving about in front, and the shore lined with children wading in the water and building their castles on the sands. Towards noon dinner was served in the assembly-room at the Clifton Arms Hotel, and the party assembled there in charge of Mr. Edmondson, the schoolmaster, Miss Clarke, the schoolmistress, and Mr. Jas. Clarke, the organist and choir master of Singleton Church. An excellent dinner was served, and all the wants of the little folks were kindly and efficiently attended to by T. H. Miller, Esq., and Mrs. T. H. Miller, W. P. Miller, Esq. (of Merlewood and Thistleton), and Mrs. W. P. Miller, Mrs. Miller, Miss Miller, Rev. L. C. Wood (Vicar of Singleton), Mrs. T. Townley Parker, Miss Wood, and Miss Clark. In the afternoon an adjournment was made to the Lytham Cricket Club ground, and sports of various kinds took place, prizes of all descriptions being awarded to the successful competitors. These prizes were presented by the several members of Mrs. Miller's family, and consisted of books, writing cases, and other useful articles. In course of the day also, the members of the choir went down to St. John's Church yard to visit the grave of the late T. Miller, Esq., and whilst there they went, by permission, into the church, and Mr. J. Rainford, the organist of St. John's, having kindly allowed Mr. Jas. Clarke to open the organ, the Singleton choir sang Helmer's Te Deum, and were very much pleased indeed with the fine instrument by which they were accompanied. Towards five o'clock, tea was served at the Clifton Arms, and after another hour or two pleasantly passed in wandering about the town, the party started again for home at seven o'clock, cheering loudly as they passed Mrs. Miller's house. The day was very fine throughout, and all enjoyed themselves thoroughly.

Singleton School in 1906.

Singleton School Band circa 1938 - Conductor: Sheila Carr.
Back row, left to right: Tommy ?,Peggy Morris, unknown, Annie Richardson, unknown, Elizabeth Martindale, Harry Rigby.
Front row, left to right: Ada Kirkham, Stan Parkinson, John Thistlethwaite, unknown, Brian ?, Ronnie ?, Winston Parkinson, ? Carr, Norma Eaves, and Buster Carr seated at the front.

School photo from the late 1970s. With teacher Mrs Asquith were - *front row, left to right*: Elaine Kay, Amanda Warren, Samantha Barnes, Nicola Manton, Joanne Taziker. *Middle row, left to right* - Julia Falkner, Maureen Brown, Rebecca Chew, Vicky Snell. *Back row, left to right*: Julian Wood, Giles Uppard, Simon Duncan, Philip Smith, Darren Edmondson.

Newspaper cutting referring to an oak tablet being unveiled at the school to commemorate fallen heroes of the First World War.

SINGLETON.

An oak tablet on the wall in Singleton School, erected in memory of the old scholars who fell in the Great War, was unveiled on Sunday afternoon by Mrs. T. H. Miller. There was a large attendance of scholars, parents, and old scholars. The impressive service was conducted by the Vicar, the Rev. T. H. Watson, M.A., who, in a short address, said the tablet served two purposes. It was there as a memorial to the fallen, and as an inspiration to the living to do their duty.

'School House', next door to the school, and so called because the headmaster lived there. The last to live there, from 1905 to 1930, was Mr. Thomas Dawson. The house subsequently became the residence of the church verger, until the last one retired several years ago. It remains under the ownership of the Singleton Trust and is rented out as a family home.

View of Miller Crescent, its houses completed in the early 1960s.

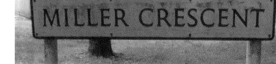

The picturesque church of St. Anne, nestling among trees along Church Road is, considered by many, to be the perfect location for a traditional village wedding.

One of the earliest records of a church in Singleton dates from 1358 and refers to a St. Mary's Chapel, described as a *'low building with a thatched roof and the eaves reaching almost to the ground'*.

In 1809 Joseph Hornby of Ribby, who was at that time Lord of the Manor of Singleton, replaced the chapel at a cost of around £4,000. This new building was described as *'a neat Gothic style church with a square tower and a peal of six bells'*.

Our present church, with seating for 300, was erected with money given by Alderman Thomas Miller and consecrated in 1860. After the death of Alderman Miller in 1865, his son, Thomas Horrocks Miller, took a great interest in the church: it was he who provided the lychgate, in 1879. Many of the wall plaques within the church commemorate members of the Miller family.

INCUMBENTS OF SINGLETON

1358	John de Est Witton
About 1545	Richard Godson
About 1562	Thomas Fieldhouse
1651	Cuthbert Harrison, B.A.
1749	John Threlfall, B.A.
About 1809	Thomas Banks
1842	William Birley, B.A.
1843	Leonard Charles Wood, B.A.
1912	Creswell Strange, M.A.
1919	Thomas Herman Watson, M.A.
1944	Joseph Brittain Goodall, M.A., Canon of Blackburn

The present Churchwardens are Mr. T. Cowell and Mr. R. H. Richardson; the Choirmaster and Organist, Mr. S. W. Mapp; and the Sunday School Superintendent, Mrs. M. Kirkham.

The Font Ewer was presented by William Kenyon to commemorate the Baptism of John Allen Parkinson in 1899.

New Hymn Books for the use of the congregation and choir were given by Mr. John Loftus and Mrs. Loftus, Snr., in 1952.

The Oak Table at the West end of the Church was made and purchased in 1953 to commemorate the Coronation of Queen Elizabeth II.

The Churchwardens' staves were the gift of Commander C. F. B. Powell, R.N., in 1956.

The Sunday School has a large and handsome Banner made in 1958 by the Sisters of the Convent of St. Peter, Horbury, and depicts the Good Shepherd.

A list of incumbents, in a booklet about St. Anne's Church published in 1960 to commemorate the centenary.

Interior of St. Anne's Church before the installation of electric lights, showing the old oil lights. The church has some beautiful stained glass windows, three of which were presented in 1860, as was the stone font, given by Mary Cairns, sister of Thomas Miller.

Another feature of the church is the large number of stone carvings and gargoyles - 71 altogether! - on the outside of the building in the form of human faces, griffins, angels, and leaves. We understand that many stonemasons were allowed to carve faces from people they knew and even carved their own faces!

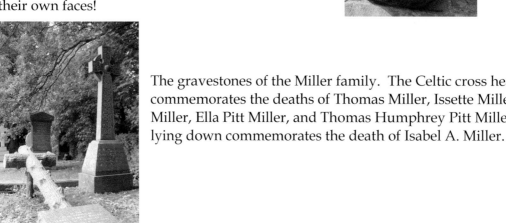

The gravestones of the Miller family. The Celtic cross headstone commemorates the deaths of Thomas Miller, Issette Miller, Thomas Pitt Miller, Ella Pitt Miller, and Thomas Humphrey Pitt Miller. The cross lying down commemorates the death of Isabel A. Miller.

View of the church from the *'Puzzle Garden'* across the road in the early 1900s. A pathway from Singleton Park leads through the gardens to the church.

View from the back of the church showing the peaceful graveyard flanked by open fields. Leading from the back of the churchyard is a secluded footpath to Mile Road, a shortcut to church for the parishioners there.

A beautiful cockerel weathervane tops the church tower.

Newspaper cutting dated May 1925 reporting the funeral of Mr. John Hull, *'an old and highly-esteemed Singleton resident'*.

SINGLETON.

The funeral took place at the Singleton Parish Church, on Thursday afternoon, of the late Mr. John Hull, an old and highly-esteemed Singleton resident. The Rev. R. W. M. Holme, Vicar of Weeton, officiated.

Mr. Hull, who was 76 years of age, was for a considerable number of years a gardener at Singleton Park. Before coming to Singleton he was in the Army, and had served in China. His death on Sunday, after a short illness, caused deep regret in the village.

In addition to the family mourners at the funeral were the following: Mr. F. N. Percival (representing Mrs. T. H. Miller, Singleton Park), Mr. Arthur Wood, Mr. John Cowell, Mr. and Mrs. Crossley. Acting as bearers were workmen from the Park.

Wreaths were received from the following:—

His sorrowing wife; Alice, and Ernest and daughter, Millicent; Arthur, Beatrice and grandson, Annie, Jim and little James; Mrs. T. H. Miller (Singleton Park); Mr. and Mrs. Cowell (Pitfield Farm); Sarah (Blackpool); from his daughter-in-law and grandchildren (Blackpool); "Little Alice."

This is the base of a stone cross, now next to the front porch of St. Anne's Church, which was probably a boundary stone originally set on the nearby roadside by the monks of Cockersand Abbey.

Datestone showing the initials of the Reverend Thomas Herman Watson and his wife Mary Alexander (nee Silcock). Thomas Watson was the Vicar of Singleton from 1919 to 1944 and '*Long Leys*' was especially built for him and his bride in

1928 in the style of his wife's family home at Thornton. *'Long Leys'* was the third building in the village to become a vicarage. After the Rev. Watson died, little Tommy Humphrey Pitt Miller and his mother Ella lived in *'Long Leys'* and were looked after by Jimmy Riley and his wife. The house is now divided into two homes, one still called *'Long Leys'* and the other called *'Applegarth'*.

More stone sculptures to be found on St. Anne's Church.

View looking west along '*Sandy Lane*'. The lane has been called this by the locals for a number of years but whether it got its name from the amount of sand in the soil at the beginning of the lane, we will never know. The lane is almost certainly medieval: it ran from *'The Grange'* to *'Bankfield'* and the banks of the River Wyre.

1910 map showing all the places of interest in Singleton.

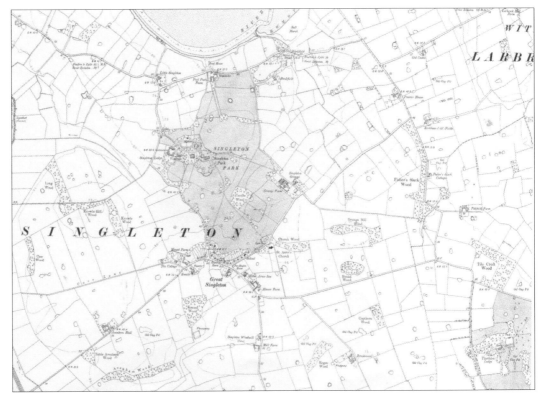

One of Singleton's two milestones, date unknown. This one is in Poolfoot Lane, which was the main road between Poulton and Garstang before the present Garstang Road was built. It shows, on the left-hand side, the distance to Gt. Eccleston (2 3/4 miles), Garstang (9 1/4 miles) and Lancaster (20 miles). The other side shows the distance to Poulton-le-Fylde (3 1/4 miles) and Blackpool (7 miles). The other milestone is one mile further west, on Mains Lane.

In 1774, Grange Farm, containing 94 acres, became part of the Great Singleton Estate when purchased, from the Fayle family, for £3,900 by William Cunliffe Shawe. The farmhouse and a barn were rebuilt in the Hornby era. During the Miller squirarchy it became the estate *'home farm'* with a new set of farm buildings. It was stocked with a flock of Shropshire sheep, and a herd of 50 cows - 34 cross-bred shorthorns and 16 Jerseys. A *'model'* dairy, built adjoining the farmhouse, was fitted with *'state of the art'* equipment. Courses on butter-making were held for Lancashire farmers' wives.

Following the sale by Adam Eccleston, grandson of the 1543 purchaser of Singleton Grange, a long process of fragmentation began as sections of the monastic estate were bought and sold separately. In 1614 the Rev. William Leigh, a rector of Standish, chaplain to the Duchy and a noted preacher, bought the bulk of the estate and his eldest son, Theophilus, came to live at Singleton Grange. During the family occupancy the land was mortgaged and re-mortgaged and parts were sold. The Leighs lived at Singleton and a Preston house until the time of William's great grandson, Dr. Charles Leigh, a physician and natural history author: Leigh died, childless, in the early 1700s leaving what little of the Singleton Grange he still owned heavily mortgaged.

By the end of the 18th century the bulk of the estate belonged to the Harrisons of Bankfield. It was their heir, Charles Edwards Dyson Harrison Atkinson, who was responsible for the present-day appearance of Singleton Grange farmhouse, presumably adapted by him to create a home for himself and his mother. Though little used by him following her death, it remained his Singleton home until he died in 1937.

'*Mains Hall*', from a sketch dated 1853. The earliest surviving Mains Hall document records its purchase, in 1602, by William Hesketh of Little Poulton, from the Earls of Derby. It was his family home until 1751, when, because of inheritance problems, the family name was changed to Brockholes and the principal family dwelling became Claughton Hall, near Garstang. Mains Hall Estate remained in Brockholes, later Fitzherbert-Brockholes, hands until divided into lots and sold in 1915.

This 18th century dovecote is one of very few in Lancashire (one is at Gt. Eccleston and another at Lytham Hall): it stands in the field on the north side of Mains Hall, between the house and the River Wyre. It is an octagonal structure of hand-made brick, which had a pointed roof until at least 1916, but is now roofless. The interior is lined with rows of nest holes (around 500) with continuous perching ledges beneath each row. Dovecotes were used in Tudor times to collect eggs from doves and pigeons to supplement a limited diet: presumably when the birds were older they were eaten as well.

An aerial view of Mains Hall taken in the middle of the 20th Century and showing the hall, its farm buildings, and the drive from Mains Lane. The large barn to the east of the house is dated 1686 and bears the initials of Thomas and Margaret Hesketh. Its upper storey, once reached by an external staircase, contained the domestic chapel which, as described by the Reverend Thornber, who visited in 1845/6, then contained decaying ecclesiastical fittings and a picture of the Virgin and Child.

The oldest building in the complex once stood to the west of the house: demolished in the first quarter of the nineteenth century it had consisted of butteries, kitchen, and oak-panelled great hall. Priest holes were discovered within the walls when they were demolished. The house in the centre, originally built to face the River Wyre and retaining a tree-lined drive down to its banks, has undergone numerous alterations over the centuries. Following its use as a family home it eventually became a farmhouse and then a hotel but has now reverted to family home. A modern timber-framed building, *'The Great Hall at Mains'*, has been built to replace the original and is used as a wedding and conference venue.

Fletchers' riverside campsite, on Mains Lane, pictured before the Second World War. One could hire a bungalow with bedding (except sheets), cooking stove, utensils (except cutlery) for 17/6d per head per week. Canvas-topped bungalows were cheaper, at 10 shillings a head, and tent rates were 6d per head nightly!

'Bankfield House', a late Georgian house destroyed by fire on 29th September 1963, only two weeks before it and its 454 acre estate were due to be sold at auction!

Originally part of Cockersand Abbey's Singleton grange, it was under the tenancy and then ownership of the Harrison family from the 1620s: they expanded the estate by buying more ex-grange land and farms Over Wyre. Seven generations of Harrisons occupied a dwelling at Bankfield until 1850 when the heiress, Agnes Elizabeth, died childless. She left Bankfield to her husband, Edwards Atkinson, JP of Fleetwood, who remarried and had three children: the elder son Charles Edwards Dyson Harrison Atkinson inherited Bankfield. In 1937 Charles died childless and Bankfield passed to his eldest nephew, Henry Gladstone Harrison Atkinson, the 51-year-old head of a Chicago advertising agency. During their ownership the Atkinson family spent some time at Bankfield, but mostly it was rented out.

In October 1963 the auction went ahead, despite the fire damage. A subsequent owner replaced the burned-out mansion with a contemporary house.

Newspaper cutting regarding the forthcoming auction of Bankfield Manor.

BLAZE HITS OLD MANOR

CCENTURIES-OLD Bankfield Manor,' at Singleton, near Blackpool, which was badly damaged by a mystery fire, will be auctioned on October 10 as arranged.

Auctioneer Mr. Peter Bibby said to-day it was too late to cancel the arrangements, and that the Manor might not be as extensively damaged as was first thought.

He said the house was only part of the 330-acre estate, which included four farms.

The owner is an American, 70-year-old Mr. Henry Gladstone Atkinson, who lives in Chicago.

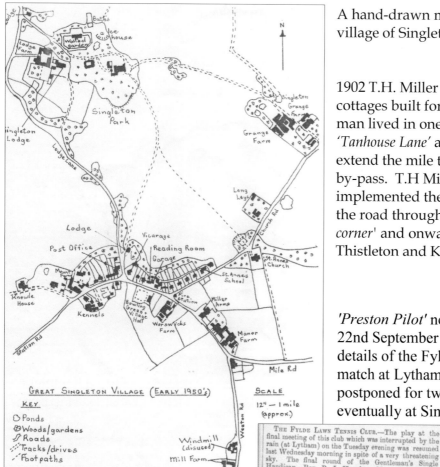

A hand-drawn map, from the early 1950s, of the village of Singleton.

1902 T.H. Miller datestone on the Mile Road cottages built for Estate workers. The pest control man lived in one. Mile Road was originally called *'Tanhouse Lane'* and did not extend the mile to the present by-pass. T.H Miller implemented the extension of the road through to 'Hell-fire corner' and onwards to Thistleton and Kirkham.

'Preston Pilot' newspaper cutting, dated 22nd September 1880, announcing details of the Fylde Lawn Tennis Club match at Lytham which was then postponed for two weeks and to be held eventually at Singleton Park.

THE FYLDE LAWN TENNIS CLUB.—The play at the final meeting of this club which was interrupted by the rain (at Lytham) on the Tuesday evening was resumed last Wednesday morning in spite of a very threatening sky. The final round of the Gentleman's Single Handicap—Rev. P. J. Hornby v. Mr. A. R. Percival—in which each had won one set, was concluded, the Rev. P. J. Hornby being the winner. Some of the sets in the Ladies' and Gentlemen's Double Prize were commenced, but rain again set in so persistently that the play had to be suspended after one or two of the more adventurous were thoroughly wet, and the concluding of the meeting was postponed for a fortnight, to take place at Singleton Park, the residence of T. H. Miller, Esq.

Card announcing a Grand Concert to be held on 6th March 1903 on behalf of Singleton Cricket Club. This card and two others have remained on a wooden wall in the Estate's workshop ever since!

1984 photo of the Singleton Bellringers - *back row, from left to right*: Martin Bankier, Ellen Goodier, David Loftus, Tom Robson, Bob Brown, Leonard Goodier; *front row, from left to right*: Hannah Loftus, Norma Clark, Ann Loftus, Jean Redmayne, Olive Robson, Val Woods, Alan Woods, Alan Smith, Edward Redmayne.

SINGLETON.

A party, numbering 34, members of the Singleton Church Choir and workers went to London on Tuesday. They had a strenuous day, but "it was worth it," they afterwards declared. A special 'bus took them to Blackpool Central Station for the 12-5 a.m. train. They reached London about 6 a.m., and their programme for the day was as follows: Breakfast at Strand "Corner House"; Hyde Park, Buckingham Palace, Westminster Abbey. Lunch at "Corner House" (saw King and Queen of Rumania pass in state down the Stran). Afternoon and evening at Wembley. Leaving London at midnight, they arrived at Kirkham at 5-30 on Wednesday morning, where a special 'bus was in waiting to convey them to Singleton. Mr. S. W. Mapp, organist and choirmaster, arranged the outing.

1930s newspaper cutting reporting the Singleton church choir's trip to London, organised by organist and choirmaster Stephen Mapp.

1930s photo of Singleton choir, once again enjoying themselves on a coach trip.

Two 'lengthsmen' (road workers), pausing to have their photograph taken in Singleton in the 1880s. The gentleman with the spade is Robert Eastham.

Singleton Home Guard, or 'Dads Army'. The only person we recognise is Edward Martindale (third on the left).

More wonderful sculptures on St. Anne's Church. The one on the left is wearing a bishop's mitre.

The 1938 Singleton Rose Queen, Lynda Gardner, and her retinue. Left to right they are: Dorothy Miller, Ronnie Parker, Annie Richardson, Herbert Richardson, Tommy Ronson, Hazel Kirkham, Lynda Gardner, Rose Queen Norma Eaves, Lucy Kirkham, Elizabeth Martindale, Bill Richardson, Sheila Carr, and Tom Swarbrick.

1924	Alice Swift	1933	Agnes Rich
1925	Isabel Clark	1934	Maud Swift
1926	Marjorie Wilson	1935	Eleanor Smith
1927	Alice Southworth	1936	Alice Smith
1928	Minnie Danson	1937	Joan Clarkson
1929	Agnes Bergus	1938	Lynda Gardner
1930	Betty Rich	1939	Elsie Turner
1931	Annie Drinkwater	1940	Margaret Thistlethwaite
1932	Dorothy Parkinson		

1924 was the first year that Singleton had a Rose Queen: she was crowned at the Annual Club Day in Singleton Park. The tradition continued until 1940. All the Rose Queens between 1924 and 1940 are listed on the left.

1930 newspaper cutting reporting the events at Singleton Gala Day.

SINGLETON.

Singleton Club Day has been fixed for Wednesday, June 4th. The programme will include the usual procession, Rose Queen coronation and sports.

Betty Rich, of Oldcastle Farm, Singleton, has been chosen as Rose Queen by the elder scholars of the village school, which she attends. Betty, who is twelve years old, will be crowned by Mrs. T. Dawson, the wife of the local schoolmaster.

Singleton Rose Queen (1934) Maud Swift and her retinue, who are, left to right of those we know: Leslie Smith, Evelyn Swift, Dorothy Pilling, Herbert Richardson, Kathleen Holden, Maud Swift, Jack Martindale, Gladys Waring, Margaret Thistlethwaite, Marie Mapp, Sheila Gardner, and Jean Jackson.

In 1951 the Singleton and Thistleton Gala was revived and became a traditional annual event until 1993, when it was sadly disbanded.

The two small pictures are of the 1936 gala.

Singleton Gala 1936

The following is a list of all the Rose Queens from 1951 to 1993: (see page 67)

1951	Shirley Conway	1958	Sheila Brayshaw	1965	Judith Miller
1952	Mary Singleton	1959	Doreen Marrison	1966	Carolyn Miller
1953	Edna Strong	1960	Christine Partington	1967	Pat Lee
1954	Margaret Eaves	1961	Maxine Miller	1968	Elaine Brownwood
1955	Ann Houghton	1962	Christine Singleton	1969	Mary Ireland
1956	Jean Wood	1963	Jackie Burns	1970	Susan McKenzie
1957	Bryony Silcock	1964	Janet Chew	1971	Jackie Moor

The 1951 Rose Queen, Shirley Conway, and her retinue. Pictured from the left they are: John Chew (Prince Charming), Audrey Tootal, Shirley Conway, Sheila Brayshaw and Janet Simmons.

List of all the Rose Queens from 1951 to 1993 (see page 66)

1972	Jayne Hargreaves	1979	Maria Ward	1986	Julie Taziker
1973	Jane Hargreaves	1980	Louise Holmes	1987	Wendy Snell
1974	Janet Ronson	1981	Joanne Highton	1988	Jennifer Kinder
1975	Wendy Miller	1982	Amanda Crompton	1989	Kendra Pemberton
1976	Debbie Richardson	1983	Joanne Taziker	1990	Charlotte Bonney
1977	Gail Hodgson	1984	Maureen Brown	1991	Elizabeth Bonney
1978	Wendy Edmondson	1985	Tara Thornburrow	1992	Ashleigh Richardson
				1993	Donna Riding

In 1999 a new committee decided to hold a Village Fayre Day on the school field. This is now an annual event, held on the third Sunday in June, which maintains the traditional country gala with a Rose Queen, clog dancing, maypole, fancy dress, a band and sports.
The following are the Rose Queens from 1999:

1999	Laura Slack	2003	Bethany Grey	2007	Lucy Wilman
2000	Francesca Britton	2004	Amy Taziker	2008	Alicia Eland
2001	Abby Pridmore	2005	Lauren Taziker	2009	Emily Grey
2002	Kimberley Braithwaite	2006	Hattie Pridmore		

Singleton Gala Committee on Coronation Day 1937. *Back row, left to right*: Bill Dixon, Alf Southworth, Jack Miller, Mr. Rigby, Mr. Stupples, Mr. Percival, Mr. Mapp, Mr. J. Martindale. *Front row, left to right*: Bill Martindale, unknown, Mrs. Issette Miller, Rev. Watson, and Mr. Richardson.

Front cover of the Singleton and Thistleton Gala and Sports programme for 1983.

Procession through the village at Singleton Gala in 1961, with Rose Queen Maxine Miller (now Chew) on her horse-drawn float.

Singleton Cloggers in 1961. Kathleen Evans (now Angel) was the Leader and had roped in a few of her friends from Hodgson School - all girls! Those we know the names of are, from left to right: Pam Schofield (now Hawthornthwaite), Susan Gregson (now Wilding), Pat Riley, Carolyn Mellows-Facer, and Brenda Cross.
Pam Schofield seems to have told a joke which has caused some smirks and smiles!

Singleton Cloggers in 1953 or 1954. Men were in short demand then, so Olive Highton (third from the left) had to don some breeches.

Richard Dumbreck, seen here, the great grandson of Alderman Thomas Miller, was born in 1914. He was educated at Charterhouse and Cambridge University. He served with the Royal Artillery in the Second World War in various theatres of war. He became the owner and head teacher of a boy's preparatory school near Tumbridge Wells.

Photographed in 1992 when Worswick's Cottages were being built. These cottages stand on what was Worswick's Farm, named after an early tenant, opposite the fire station.

The back of farm buildings at Worswick's Farm before their renovation and the cows were re-housed!

He inherited the Singleton Estate in 1963, upon the death of Tommy Miller, and to quote his own words *"by a somewhat devious route"* because of the breakdown of the direct male line. Although a somewhat absentee landlord because of his commitments in Sussex, he kept an eye on Singleton and was keen that it should prosper as a community. To this end he left instructions in his will that, upon his death, his executors were to set up a charitable trust to hold the estate for the benefit of the village and its community. He died on 21st January 2003.

The trust which bears his name is administered by a group of trustees with the day-to-day running of the estate entrusted to a firm of surveyors and land agents. The trustees are committed to improving the cottages in the village and bringing them up to modern standards. They are particularly proud of the 2008 conversion of the redundant farm buildings at Worswick's Farm into six self-contained dwellings around a centre courtyard. The development has been named *'Dumbreck Court'* as a memorial to Richard.

The rear of the farm buildings at Worswick's Farm (now *'Dumbreck Court'*, as previously mentioned), at exactly the same spot where the cow pictured on the previous page was housed.

General view from the front of Dumbreck Court.

71

Singleton Girl Guides on a camping trip to the Lakes in the 1940s. Dorothy Miller is 3rd from right on the front row, and Norma Eaves is directly behind.

They held their weekly meetings in the Village Hall. The Brownie pack also met in Singleton, meeting initially in the Reading Room.

Letter, dated 2nd May 1949, from the National Federation of Women's Institutes welcoming the members of Singleton Women's Institute.

There has been a Women's Institute in Singleton since May 1949. That first meeting saw a membership of 42. Over the years, numbers have fluctuated but there is still a warm and friendly atmosphere at the monthly meetings, held in the same hall since it began. The W.I. celebrated its Diamond Anniversary in May 2009 with a dinner at Singleton Lodge.

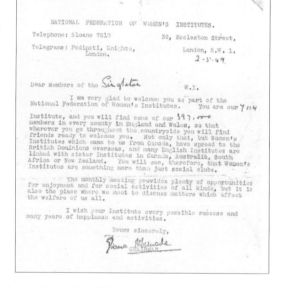

The Village Hall has been described by several names, first as the Parochial Hall, then as the Church Hall. Built in 1924, it has been 'home' to the Guides, Brownies, Women's Institute, Crown Green Bowling Club, Mothers' Union, Youth Club, concerts, dancing, and Singleton Parish Council.